OECD/G20 Base Erosion and Profit Shifting Project

Pillar One - Amount B

INCLUSIVE FRAMEWORK ON BEPS

OECD
BETTER POLICIES FOR BETTER LIVES

This document, as well as any data and map included herein, are without prejudice to the status of or sovereignty over any territory, to the delimitation of international frontiers and boundaries and to the name of any territory, city or area.

Please cite this publication as:
OECD (2024), *Pillar One - Amount B: Inclusive Framework on BEPS*, OECD/G20 Base Erosion and Profit Shifting Project, OECD Publishing, Paris, https://doi.org/10.1787/21ea168b-en.

ISBN 978-92-64-93319-4 (print)
ISBN 978-92-64-62283-8 (PDF)
ISBN 978-92-64-64711-4 (HTML)

OECD/G20 Base Erosion and Profit Shifting Project
ISSN 2313-2604 (print)
ISSN 2313-2612 (online)

Revised version, May 2026
Details of revisions available at: https://www.oecd.org/about/publishing/corrigenda.htm

Photo credits: © ninog – Fotolia.com.

Corrigenda to OECD publications may be found at: https://www.oecd.org/en/publications/support/corrigenda.html.

Foreword

In an increasingly globalised economy, multinational enterprises operate expansive value chains spanning several countries. As a result, lengthy cross-border tax disputes may arise, especially in relation to baseline marketing and distribution activities. These disputes often drain the financial and administrative resources of all parties involved. This challenge is only amplified for low-capacity jurisdictions whose tax administrations often grapple with limited resources and unavailable data. This report provides guidance designed to simplify the application of transfer pricing rules with regards to baseline marketing and distribution activities, alleviate administrative burden, cut compliance costs, and enhance tax certainty for tax administrations and taxpayers alike.

Released in October 2020, the OECD/G20 Inclusive Framework on Base Erosion and Profit Shifting report *Tax Challenges Arising from Digitalisation – Report on Pillar One Blueprint* stated that Amount B was intended to simplify and streamline the application of the arm's length principle to baseline marketing and distribution activities, with a focus on the specific needs of low-capacity jurisdictions. In October 2021, the Inclusive Framework agreed a two-pillar solution to address the tax challenges arising from the digitalisation of the economy.

For the past two years, Inclusive Framework members have worked on an equal footing to ensure that Amount B delivers meaningful simplification to price baseline marketing and distribution activities, considering in particular the challenges that low-capacity jurisdictions face in applying transfer pricing. In designing Amount B, the Inclusive Framework has benefited from businesses, tax practitioners, academics, and other stakeholders' inputs through the public consultations held in December 2022 and July 2023. As a key deliverable of Pillar One, Amount B is expected to not only provide relief of compliance burdens for taxpayers but also to enable tax administrations to allocate resources towards riskier and more complex transactions, thereby ensuring a more efficient and impactful approach to their work.

This report was approved and declassified by the Inclusive Framework.[1]

Table of contents

Executive Summary

In October 2021, the OECD/G20 Inclusive Framework on Base Erosion and Profit Shifting (Inclusive Framework) agreed to simplify and streamline the application of the arm's length principle to in-country baseline marketing and distribution activities, with a particular focus on the needs of low-capacity jurisdictions. Following that mandate, this report contains the guidance on "Special considerations for baseline distribution activities" which is incorporated into the *OECD Transfer Pricing Guidelines for Multinational Enterprises and Tax Administrations 2022* as an Annex to Chapter IV. The simplified and streamlined approach set out in that guidance is expected to enhance tax certainty and to relieve compliance burdens for taxpayers and tax administrations alike, particularly those in low-capacity jurisdictions facing limited resources.

Jurisdictions can choose to apply the simplified and streamlined approach to qualifying transactions of eligible baseline distributors. The guidance in this report sets out the characteristics of in-scope distributors, which cannot, for example, assume certain economically significant risks or own unique and value intangibles. Moreover, certain activities may exclude a distributor from the scope, such as the distribution of commodities or digital goods. The simplified and streamlined approach provides a pricing framework whereby a 3-step process determines a return on sales for in-scope distributors. Finally, the report also provides guidance on documentation, transitional issues, and tax certainty considerations.

Introduction

In its Statement of October 2021, the OECD/G20 Inclusive Framework on Base Erosion and Profit Shifting (Inclusive Framework) agreed to simplify and streamline the application of the arm's length principle to in-country baseline marketing and distribution activities, with a particular focus on the needs of low-capacity jurisdictions. In July 2023, the Inclusive Framework agreed to publish a final Amount B report, content from which would be incorporated into the *OECD Transfer Pricing Guidelines for Multinational Enterprises and Tax Administrations 2022* by January 2024 with due consideration given to both the needs of low-capacity jurisdictions, and the interdependence of Amount B with the signing and entry into force of the Multilateral Convention to Implement Amount A of Pillar One ("MLC").[2]

This report responds to the mandate of the Inclusive Framework by providing an optional simplified and streamlined approach – formerly referred to as Amount B – that jurisdictions can choose to apply to in-scope distributors resident in their jurisdictions.[3] It reflects the consensus of the Inclusive Framework and takes account of comments received in response to the public consultation documents released on 8 December 2022 and on 17 July 2023. As part of the current workstream, the Inclusive Framework is working on an additional optional qualitative scoping criterion that jurisdictions may choose to apply as an additional step to identify distributors performing non-baseline activities for the purpose of the simplified and streamlined approach. The Inclusive Framework will conclude this work by 31st March 2024, with any additions to be incorporated into the OECD Transfer Pricing Guidelines.[4]

The simplified and streamlined approach draws from the general principles outlined in the OECD Transfer Pricing Guidelines and is incorporated into the OECD Transfer Pricing Guidelines as an Annex to Chapter IV. Notably, nothing in the guidance contained in this report should be construed as a basis to interpret the application of the general principles in the remainder of the OECD Transfer Pricing Guidelines with respect to any transactions, nor should this guidance be interpreted as revising those principles. Following the publication of this report, jurisdictions can choose to apply the simplified and streamlined approach for in-scope transactions of tested parties in their jurisdictions for fiscal years commencing on or after 1 January 2025.

Jurisdictions can choose to apply the simplified and streamlined approach to the qualifying transactions of their in-scope tested parties according to the options articulated in Section 2 of this report. Similar to other elective approaches in the OECD Transfer Pricing Guidelines, the outcome determined under the simplified and streamlined approach by a jurisdiction that has chosen to apply the simplified and streamlined approach to qualifying transactions of its in-scope tested party is non-binding on the counter-party jurisdiction where the associated enterprise that is a party to the controlled transaction is located. However, subject to their domestic legislations and administrative practices, members of the Inclusive Framework commit to respect the outcome determined under the simplified and streamlined approach to in-scope transactions where such approach is applied by a low-capacity jurisdiction[5] and to take all reasonable steps to relieve potential double taxation that may arise from the application of the simplified and streamlined approach by a low-capacity jurisdiction where there is a bilateral tax treaty in effect between the relevant jurisdictions.[6] The Inclusive Framework will work on the implementation of this commitment in 2024, including through the development of competent authority agreements that could be used within the context of bilateral tax treaty relationships, taking into consideration the dual objective of bilateral tax treaties to avoid double taxation, as well as to prevent double non-taxation. The Inclusive Framework will agree on the design elements and on the list of low-capacity jurisdictions within scope of this commitment by consensus in 2024. The Inclusive Framework will agree on the list of low-capacity jurisdictions by 31 March 2024.[7]

Section 3 of this report describes and defines the set of qualifying transactions within scope of this simplified and streamlined approach, and consequently the characteristics of in-scope distributors. In-scope distributors, for instance, should not own unique and valuable intangibles nor should they assume certain economically significant risks. The simplified and streamlined approach allows in-scope distributors to perform non-distribution transactions when they can be adequately evaluated and reliably priced on a separate basis under the general principles of the OECD Transfer Pricing Guidelines. It also permits the undertaking of *de minimis* retail sales, while excluding the distribution of digital goods, commodities and services from scope.

Section 4 of this report explains the relationship of this simplified and streamlined approach to the most appropriate method principle, and Section 5 sets forth a 3-step process for determining a return on sales for an in-scope distributor which provides an approximation of an arm's length result. This pricing framework includes a matrix of returns[8]; an operating expense cross-check mechanism[9]; and a data availability mechanism.[10] [11] Sections 6 and 7 deal with documentation and transitional issues while Section 8 discusses tax certainty and the elimination of double taxation.

The Inclusive Framework directs Working Party 1 to develop text for inclusion in the commentary on Article 25 of the OECD Model Tax Convention to provide appropriate signposts to the agreed wording of this report, in particular in Section 8. Working Party 1 would work on the development of these changes in 2024 with the aim of including them in the next update of the OECD Model Tax Convention.

The Inclusive Framework will gather information on the practical application of the simplified and streamlined approach once it has been in operation for a period of time. The framework to gather such information will be developed in 2024.[12] The design of such framework will build on information available from jurisdictions' current reporting requirements and audit practices and account for the resources needed to undertake this exercise. Therefore, it should not impose an unreasonable administrative burden on tax administrations. In addition, consideration could be given to produce further implementation guidance, as needed.

Notes

[1] Note by India: India wishes to record its reservation on the incomplete nature of the report owing to the non-inclusion of the definitions of 'low-capacity jurisdictions (LCJs) and 'qualifying jurisdictions'; and an appropriately designed optional qualitative scoping criterion. Further, India also wishes to record its reservation on various aspects of the Amount B design, including but not limited to the operating expense cross-check mechanism and the overall design of the pricing methodology. The detailed reservations are incorporated as footnotes within the report.

[2] OECD (2023), Outcome Statement on the Two-Pillar Solution to Address the Tax Challenges Arising from the Digitalisation of the Economy – 11 July 2023 (https://www.oecd.org/tax/beps/outcome-statement-on-the-two-pillar-solution-to-address-the-tax-challenges-arising-from-the-digitalisation-of-the-economy-july-2023.htm).

[3] The content of this report, including any design elements, should be considered without prejudice to any future work on Amount B, such as on the interdependence of Amount B with the signing and entry into force of the MLC.

[4] Note by India: India believes that an appropriately designed qualitative criterion is critical to ensure that only baseline distributors are in scope of Amount B. India expresses inability to support the Amount B work further if such a criterion is not incorporated as part of the scoping criteria in this report.

[5] The list of low-capacity jurisdictions considered for these purposes will be made available on the OECD website.

[6] Some members of the Inclusive Framework may be able and willing under their domestic legislations and administrative procedures to extend this commitment to cases where no bilateral tax treaty exists.

[7] Note by India: India expresses its inability to make a political commitment in respect of an undefined set of jurisdictions termed as "LCJ" in an incomplete Amount B report. India believes that the report should be completed and the definition of "LCJs" should be agreed before the issue of political commitment is taken up.

[8] Note by India: India records its reservation on the design elements of the pricing methodology, including but not limited to, the exclusion of goodwill from the intangible fixed assets for calculating net operating assets of a tested party, the wide deviation range of +/-0.5% vis-à-vis the median that has been allowed for each cell of the pricing matrix, the design of pricing matrix through use of a single commercial database that has not yielded a geographically representative dataset, the appropriateness of the filtering criteria, the factor used in matrix and their categorisation.

[9] Note by India: India expresses its in-principal objection to the use of an operating expense based metric as a cross-check to cap (or collar) the return of the distributors under Amount B. India considers that the value of a distributor's functional contributions is reflected in the sales made by it, and not in the operating expense of the distributor. India also believes that the cross-check could adversely affect lower income countries, where it considers that the operating expense of similarly placed distributors is systemically lower than in high income countries, and that the alternative cap rates may not sufficiently address this issue.

[10] In the context of designing Amount B, the Inclusive Framework has explored several mechanisms to address geographical differences as reflected in the consultation documents of December 2022 and July 2023.

[11] Note by India: India expresses its objection to non-inclusion of an appropriate definition of 'qualifying jurisdictions' for section 5.2 and section 5.3, and to the proposal to incorporate the same at a later date.

[12] Note by India: India records its reservation on the proposal to develop a framework to gather information on the practical application of Amount B as no further details in respect of such framework have been provided. India also has concerns around the resource-intensive nature of any such exercise, especially from the point of view of capacity constrained jurisdictions.

The following sections of this report are added to the OECD Transfer Pricing Guidelines as an Annex to Chapter IV.

Special considerations for baseline distribution activities

DEFINITIONS

The following terms have the meanings set out below solely for the purposes of this guidance.

Distributor refers to wholesale distributors, sales agents, and commissionaires involved in the sale of goods. [1] Where applicable, specific references may be made to a wholesale or retail distributor, sales agent, or commissionaire.

Wholesale distribution includes distribution to any type of customer except end consumers. For the purposes of this guidance, a distributor that engages in wholesale and retail distribution is deemed to solely carry out wholesale distribution if its three-year weighted average net retail revenues do not exceed 20% of its three-year weighted average net revenues. [2]

Retail distribution is distribution to end consumers, typically through physical or online stores.

Baseline distribution refers to activities performed by distributors where such distributors act as tested parties in qualifying transactions under paragraph 10 of this guidance, and where such distributors meet the scoping criteria outlined in paragraphs 13 and 14 of this guidance.

Core distribution functions are distribution functions that are typically performed by baseline distributors, depending on the business model of the distributor, i.e. whether it is a buy-sell distributor,

[1] The scope of this guidance is limited to wholesale distribution of tangible goods and does not include services (including digital services).

[2] This threshold should be calculated on a three-year weighted average basis, for each year, for the purposes of determining whether the threshold is breached. For example, for a transaction in fiscal year *x*, the three-year weighted average threshold would be derived by (A) taking the sum of the annual retail revenue for years *x-3*, *x-2*, and *x-1*, then (B) taking the sum of the annual net revenues over the same period, and then dividing (A) by (B) to derive the appropriate percentage. Where the qualifying transaction has been in place for two years, a two-year weighted average ratio should be used, and where the qualifying transaction has been in place for only one year the ratio should be calculated based on the financial results for that year.

sales agent, or commissionaire. Core distribution functions may include buying goods for resale, identification of new customers and managing customers' relationships, certain after-sales services, implementing promotional advertising or marketing activities, warehousing goods, processing orders or performing logistics, invoicing and collection. Core distribution functions may vary in intensity and complexity and specifically exclude non-distribution activities that may render a distributor out of scope of the simplified and streamlined approach (see Section 3.3.4 of this guidance).

Non-distribution activities are economic activities that are distinct from wholesale distribution, including, for example, manufacturing, research and development, procurement or financing that are non-incidental to a qualifying transaction. Note that, strictly for the purposes of applying scoping criteria14.b, non-distribution activities include retail distribution above the *de minimis* threshold noted in the definition of wholesale distribution (in cases where this threshold is exceeded all retail distribution is treated as a non-distribution activity).

Global dataset refers to the set of companies that has been derived from a search of a commercial database containing global company financial data, without application of any geographic filter, and which in part forms the basis for the approximation of arm's length results under the simplified and streamlined approach referenced in Section 5.

Applicable accounting standards refers to any accounting standard that is permitted as a basis upon which to prepare financial statements in the jurisdiction where the tested party performing baseline distribution activities is resident, and to any other accounting standard whose use is permitted by such jurisdiction for purposes of applying the simplified and streamlined approach referenced in Section 5.

Net revenues refers to total sales revenue excluding any sales returns, allowances, and discounts, calculated in accordance with applicable accounting standards.

Earnings before interest and taxes (EBIT) refers to financial account profit before income taxes and finance income/expense. Finance income/expense includes, but it is not limited to, interest income, interest expense, and gains & losses on investments.[3] As a general matter, EBIT should not include any exceptional items that are unrelated to recurring business operations, which should be quantified in accordance with applicable accounting standards.

Return on sales refers to the ratio of EBIT to net revenues, expressed as a percentage, and calculated in accordance with applicable accounting standards.

Net operating assets refers to the tangible and intangible fixed assets plus working capital calculated on an average basis[4] for a relevant fiscal year in accordance with applicable accounting standards. Tangible fixed assets include property, plant, and equipment net of accumulated depreciation, plus land

[3] See paragraph 2.88 of these Guidelines for specific consideration which might be given to foreign exchange risks and costs associated with such foreign exchange risks and how that might be treated when calculating net revenues, cost of goods sold, and any other line items and ratios applicable in the simplified and streamlined approach. It is possible that, if the exposure is economically significant, there may be circumstances where a party assuming such risks would not meet the scoping criteria described in Section 3.2.

[4] Net operating assets calculated on an average basis means taking the sum of the net operating assets for a relevant fiscal year (i.e. the closing balance) plus the net operating assets for the preceding fiscal year (i.e. the opening balance) and dividing by two.

plus net capital leases. Intangible fixed assets include all intangible fixed assets, net of accumulated amortisation, but excluding goodwill. Working capital is the sum of stock plus debtors less creditors. [5]

Operating expenses refers to total costs excluding cost of goods sold, pass-through costs appropriately excluded under the accurate delineation of the transaction[6] and costs related to financing, investment activities or income taxes, calculated in accordance with applicable accounting standards. Moreover, operating expenses should not include any exceptional items that are unrelated to recurring business operations, which should be quantified in accordance with applicable accounting standards.

Net operating asset intensity (OAS) refers to the ratio of net operating assets to net revenue, expressed as a percentage. [7]

Operating expense intensity (OES) refers to the ratio of operating expenses to net revenue, expressed as a percentage. [8]

Industry grouping refers to the categorisation of specific industries and industry sectors in which in-scope distributors operate into three pre-defined groupings based on the observed relationships between specific industries / products and the profitability attributed to baseline distribution of those products. The categories of goods falling into each of the three industry groups are:

- Group 1 – perishable foods, grocery, household consumables, construction materials and supplies, plumbing supplies and metal.
- Group 2 – IT hardware and components, electrical components and consumables, animal feeds, agricultural supplies, alcohol and tobacco, pet foods, clothing footwear and other apparel, plastics and chemicals, lubricants, dyes, pharmaceuticals, cosmetics, health and wellbeing products, home appliances, consumer electronics, furniture, home and office supplies, printed matter, paper and packaging, jewellery, textiles hides and furs, new and used domestic vehicles, vehicle parts and supplies, mixed products and products and components not listed in group 1 or 3.

---

[5] Creditors includes third party and intercompany payable balances. For the purpose of determining creditors of the tested party and mitigating the risk of distortive credit terms, an accounts payable days guardrail of 90 days applies. See footnote 29 in Section 5 for further practical guidance.

[6] The relevance and treatment of pass-through costs is discussed further in footnote 24 of Section 3 of this guidance.

[7] This ratio should be calculated on a three-year weighted average basis, for each fiscal year, for the purposes of determining the factor intensity classification. For example, for a tested party in fiscal year *x*, the three-year weighted average ratio would be derived by (A) taking the sum of the annual net operating assets for years *x-3*, *x-2*, and *x-1*, then (B) taking the sum of the annual total net revenue over the same period, and then dividing (A) by (B) to derive the appropriate percentage. Where the qualifying transaction has been in place for two years, a two-year weighted average ratio should be used, and where the qualifying transaction has been in place for only one year the ratio should be calculated based on the financial results for that year.

[8] This ratio should be calculated on a three-year weighted average basis, for each fiscal year, for the purposes of determining whether the scoping threshold is breached and for determining the factor intensity classification. For example, for a tested party in fiscal year *x*, the three-year weighted average threshold would be derived by (A) taking the sum of the annual operating expenses for years *x-3*, *x-2*, and *x-1*, then (B) taking the sum of the annual total net revenue over the same period, and then dividing (A) by (B) to derive the appropriate percentage. Where the qualifying transaction has been in place for two years, a two-year weighted average ratio should be used, and where the qualifying transaction has been in place for only one year the ratio should be calculated based on the financial results for that year.

- Group 3 – medical machinery, industrial machinery including industrial and agricultural vehicles, industrial tools, industrial components miscellaneous supplies.

Factor intensity classification refers to the segmentation of different levels of net operating asset and operating expense intensity into five pre-defined classifications based on the observed relationships between asset and expense intensity and the profitability attributed to baseline distribution. The factor intensity classifications are defined in the pricing matrix in table 5.1 of Section 5.

Qualifying jurisdiction(s) within the meaning of Section 5.3 refers to jurisdictions where the data availability mechanism referenced in Section 5.3 applies for the purpose of determining adjusted returns for tested parties located in those aforementioned jurisdictions. The qualifying criteria will be incorporated into this guidance in a subsequent update. The list of qualifying jurisdictions for Section 5.3 purposes will be fixed prospectively based on those qualifying criteria, published and updated every 5 years on the OECD website.

Sovereign credit rating refers to the publicly available long term sovereign credit ratings periodically assigned to or re-affirmed for a jurisdiction by a recognised independent credit rating agency and relevant to Section 5.3 guidance.

Recognised independent credit rating agency(ies) refers to the following independent credit rating agencies: Moody's Investors Service, S&P Global Ratings, and Fitch Ratings and relevant to Section 5.3 guidance.

Equivalent return on operating expense refers to the return on sales of a tested party calculated in accordance with Section 5.1 and converted into a corresponding ratio of EBIT to operating expenses for the purpose of applying the operating expense cross-check in Section 5.2.

Operating expense cap refers to the maximum equivalent return on operating expense, specified in table 5.2, that the simplified and streamlined approach will produce for a given tested party in accordance with Section 5.2.

Operating expense collar refers to the minimum equivalent return on operating expense, specified in table 5.2, that the simplified and streamlined approach will produce for a given tested party in accordance with Section 5.2.

Qualifying jurisdiction(s) within the meaning of Section 5.2 refers to jurisdictions where alternative cap rates apply for the purpose of determining the operating expense cap-and-collar range for tested parties located in those aforementioned jurisdictions. The qualifying criteria will be incorporated into this guidance in a subsequent update. The list of qualifying jurisdictions for Section 5.2 purposes will be fixed prospectively based on those qualifying criteria, published and updated every 5 years on the OECD website.

*References to the **"Remainder of these Guidelines" or "these Guidelines"*** refer to the entirety of the OECD Transfer Pricing Guidelines for Multinational Enterprises and Tax Administrations, except for the guidance contained in this Annex.

References to *"**this guidance**"* refers to the entirety of this Annex, and not to the Remainder of these Guidelines.

1 Introduction

1. Distribution is a necessary function for MNE Groups in successfully realising the value created throughout the different stages of their businesses. In general, the concept of distribution is broad but, at least, encompasses the performance of core distribution activities.

2. Transfer pricing disputes with respect to baseline marketing and distribution arrangements may involve administrative challenges for tax administrations, especially of low-capacity jurisdictions, and result in a compliance burden for taxpayers. Those disputes may arise in relation to the accurate delineation of the arrangement. Disputes may also arise with respect to the pricing considerations of marketing and distribution arrangements, focusing on areas such as the selection of the transfer pricing method, the appropriateness of the benchmarking analysis (especially the identification and selection of non-domestic comparables) or, where necessary, how to make appropriate comparability adjustments.

3. The simplified and streamlined approach articulated in this guidance is grounded in Chapters I-III and takes into account Section E of Chapter IV of these Guidelines. It contains a simplified and streamlined approach to approximate an arm's length outcome for in-scope baseline marketing and distribution arrangements. It seeks to facilitate compliance, prevent transfer pricing disputes from arising and help resolve those that do arise in a more efficient manner.

4. The simplified and streamlined approach should be regarded as a simplification measure for the pricing of in-scope distribution arrangements that draws from the general principles included in the remainder of these Guidelines. The guidance in this annex should not be regarded as a revision of those general principles, nor should it be used to interpret the application of the remainder of these Guidelines with respect to any transaction.

2 Considerations regarding the application of the simplified and streamlined approach.

5. Jurisdictions have diverse backgrounds and may encounter different challenges in applying the arm's length principle. For instance, in situations where jurisdictions face capacity constraints or challenges associated with the identification of reliable sources of information, they may choose to apply the simplified and streamlined approach for distributors resident within their jurisdiction.

6. The design of the simplified and streamlined approach simplifies pricing of in-scope transactions by providing a solution that approximates an arm's length outcome within the jurisdiction of the tested party. In jurisdictions that choose to apply the simplified and streamlined approach,[9] such approach will be treated as providing an arm's length outcome. In jurisdictions that do not choose to apply the simplified and streamlined approach, such approach will not be treated as providing an arm's length outcome (including for the purposes of Article 9 of the MTC and by extension Article 25). The outcome determined under the simplified and streamlined approach by a jurisdiction is non-binding on the counter-party jurisdiction.[10]

7. A jurisdiction that chooses to apply the simplified and streamlined approach may choose to apply it using one of two options, which specify which party or parties can assert the simplified and streamlined approach.[11] Under the first option, a jurisdiction can permit tested parties resident within its jurisdiction to elect to apply the simplified and streamlined approach. Under the second option, a jurisdiction can require the use of the simplified and streamlined approach in a prescriptive manner by its tax administration and tested parties resident in the jurisdiction and, thus, the tax administration may specify that taxpayers should apply the simplified and streamlined approach where the scoping criteria are met and the tax administration would be bound to apply it under similar circumstances.

8. Regardless of the choice by a jurisdiction between the two options, competent authorities and taxpayers should consider the relevant implications for the relief of double taxation, noting the guidance in paragraphs 4.117 and 4.131 of these Guidelines, and in Section 8 of this guidance. Taxpayers should not rely on the simplified and streamlined approach to justify that a result should be treated as an arm's length outcome when filing their tax returns in jurisdictions that do not apply the simplified and streamlined

[9] The list of jurisdictions that apply the simplified and streamlined approach for tested parties within their jurisdictions will be made available on the OECD website.

[10] Note that the outcome of applying the simplified and streamlined approach may in some cases be consistent with the outcome of applying the remainder of these Guidelines.

[11] See Chapter IV of these Guidelines, in particular paragraphs 4.102 and 4.108.

approach.[12] This would be the case for filings that are made in the jurisdiction of the tested party where the jurisdiction has not adopted the simplified and streamlined approach. It would also be the case for filings in the counterparty jurisdiction where that jurisdiction has not adopted the simplified and streamlined approach, even where the tested party is in a jurisdiction that has adopted it.

9. The arm's length outcome for out-of-scope transactions should be evaluated strictly according to the principles articulated in the remainder of these Guidelines. Moreover, the fact that an activity does not qualify for the simplified and streamlined approach under this guidance should not be interpreted to mean that such activity generates lower or higher returns than is permissible under the simplified and streamlined approach or that the returns applied for in-scope taxpayers represents a "floor" or a "ceiling" for returns to distribution activities in general.

[12] See also Section 6 and Section 8 (in particular paragraph 72) of this guidance. If a taxpayer files its tax return under the simplified and streamlined approach in a jurisdiction that has not chosen to apply it, it may be the case that the relevant local reporting requirements, including documentation, are not met under that jurisdiction's domestic rules.

3 Transactions in scope

3.1. Qualifying transactions

10. The following controlled transactions are qualifying transactions for the simplified and streamlined approach:

a. Buy-sell marketing and distribution transactions where the distributor purchases goods from one or more associated enterprises for wholesale distribution to unrelated parties; and

b. Sales agency and commissionaire transactions where the sales agent or commissionaire contributes to one or more associated enterprises' wholesale distribution of goods to unrelated parties.[13]

11. An accurate delineation of the qualifying transaction should be undertaken in accordance with Chapter I of these Guidelines, considering all five comparability factors and the economically relevant characteristics of the transaction, prior to the application of the scoping criteria.[14] A qualifying transaction, as accurately delineated, will be subject to the simplified and streamlined approach when it satisfies the scoping criteria in Section 3.2. Consequently, the information obtained in the accurate delineation of the transaction is to be used to assess whether each of the scoping criteria has been met in order to determine whether a transaction will be subject to the simplified and streamlined approach.

12. The determination of whether a qualifying transaction is within scope is not driven by the adoption of specific labels, but primarily by the functions performed, assets used, and risks assumed by the parties to the qualifying transaction. While this guidance does not attempt to provide an exhaustive list of baseline marketing and distribution activities, it recognises that distributors should perform a set of core distribution functions in relation to in-scope transactions.

3.2. Scoping criteria

13. For a qualifying transaction to be in-scope of the simplified and streamlined approach:

[13] The associated enterprise that engages the sales agent or commissionaire, and which is the counterparty to the sales agent or commissionaire in the potentially qualifying transaction, must sell the goods directly to unrelated parties, i.e. without either it or the sales agent or commissionaire engaging other related parties as intermediaries between it and the unrelated party customers.

[14] Refer also to paragraph 1.34 of these Guidelines, which should be taken into account when applying the simplified and streamlined approach.

a. The qualifying transaction must exhibit economically relevant characteristics that mean it can be reliably priced using a one-sided transfer pricing method, with the distributor, sales agent or commissionaire being the tested party.[15]

b. The tested party in the qualifying transaction must not incur annual operating expenses lower than 3% or greater than an upper bound of between 20% and 30% of the tested party's annual net revenues.[16] [17]

14. For qualifying transactions that do not fall out of scope of the simplified and streamlined approach under paragraph 13, a qualifying transaction will nevertheless be out of scope if:

a. The qualifying transaction involves the distribution of non-tangible goods, services or the marketing, trading, or distribution of commodities; or

b. The tested party carries out non-distribution activities in addition to the qualifying transaction, unless the qualifying transaction can be adequately evaluated on a separate basis and can be reliably priced separately from the non-distribution activities.[18] [19]

3.3. Commentary

15. This sub-section seeks to clarify and illustrate the application of the scoping criteria to qualifying transactions.

3.3.1. Scoping criterion 13.a - The qualifying transaction must exhibit economically relevant characteristics that mean it can be reliably priced using a one-sided method, with the distributor being the tested party

16. Scoping criterion 13.a limits the application of the simplified and streamlined approach to the set of transactions that can be reliably priced using a one-sided method, with the distributor being the tested party.

17. In evaluating whether a qualifying transaction may be within the scope, determining that a two-sided transfer pricing method should not apply is particularly important. Consequently, the first scoping

---

[15] See 2.4, 2.65, 2.66, 2.126, 3.18 and 3.19. Moreover, see Chapter II, Part III, Section B for a discussion regarding the set of economically relevant circumstances under which the transactional net margin method is the most appropriate method. Section 4 of this guidance provides additional discussion on this issue in the context of determination of arm's length returns under the simplified and streamlined approach.

[16] Where the commissionaire or sales agent is not the entity making the sale, the sales of the counterparty of the commissionaire or sales agent (i.e., whichever entity makes the sale to the third-party customer) will be utilised to compute the ratio of operating expenses to sales; however, the net operating expenses of the commissionaire or sales agent are always the sole item included in the numerator of the ratios.

[17] Jurisdictions that choose to implement the simplified and streamlined approach will specify the upper bound to apply to this scoping criterion when it is originally implemented, which will be not lower than 20% and not higher than 30%.

[18] See paragraphs 3.9 - 3.12 of these Guidelines.

[19] Where a tested party in a qualifying transaction carries out non-distribution activities such that scoping criterion 14.b is required to be evaluated, the calculation of any ratios required either to determine whether that qualifying transaction is in scope, or any other ratios that are necessary in the context of the evaluation of the qualifying transaction in this guidance, should be undertaken with regard to the revenues, expenses or assets relevant to the qualifying transaction only.

criterion establishes that any in-scope distributor must exhibit economically relevant characteristics such that the qualifying transaction can be reliably priced using a one sided-method. Section 4 provides that the transactional net margin method is chosen as the most appropriate method to price in-scope transactions under the simplified and streamlined approach, with an exception where the CUP method using internal comparables can be reliably applied and the necessary information is readily available to tax administrations and taxpayers.

18. Chapter II, Part III, Section C.2.2 outlines three key economically relevant characteristics of qualifying transactions that indicate that a one-sided transfer pricing method may not be suitable to apply to establish arm's length conditions for a qualifying transaction. These should be applied to evaluate whether a qualifying transaction is suitable for the simplified and streamlined approach. The first is where the contributions of each party to the qualifying transaction are "unique and valuable", including contributions of unique and valuable intangibles (C.2.2.1).[20] The second is where the distributor and its counterparties carry out functions, use assets and assume risks in the qualifying transaction with such a degree of integration that their contributions cannot reliably be evaluated in isolation from each other (C.2.2.2). The third is where the distributor and its counterparties share the assumption of one or more economically significant risks to the transaction, or where the various economically significant risks in relation to the transaction are separately assumed by the parties, but those risks are so closely inter-related and/or correlated that the playing out of the risks of each party cannot reliably be isolated (C.2.2.3).

19. The existing examples 1 - 4 in Annex II to Chapter II of these Guidelines provide useful information with respect to the practical application of this scoping criterion.

20. Depending on the accurate delineation of the qualifying transaction, unique and valuable contributions made by a distributor may include, but are not limited to, contributions to the development, enhancement, maintenance, protection, and exploitation of any intangibles that are themselves unique and valuable in the context of the qualifying transaction. Further guidance on the ownership of, and functions, assets, and risks related to intangibles may be found in Chapter VI, Sections B.1 and B.2 of these Guidelines, together with the framework in paragraph 6.34 to be applied for analysing transactions involving intangibles. Moreover, some examples of contributions that may be important are contained in paragraph 6.56 of these Guidelines.[21] Unique and valuable contributions of this nature are equally applicable to evaluate intangibles that are self-generated or acquired by a distributor.

21. Another source of guidance that may be relevant in identifying unique and valuable contributions in the accurate delineation of the qualifying transaction is noted in paragraphs 1.169 – 1.171 of these Guidelines. This guidance notes that in certain circumstances, a regulatory license that is required to access a market, for example, may be an intangible whose value in the context of the particular transaction will depend upon several factors, including whether the license is readily available and whether it has the

---

[20] See Glossary, and paragraphs 2.126, 2.130, and 2.131-2.132. This criterion specifically applies to any situation where the contributions of the distributor to the qualifying transaction are unique and valuable.

[21] The examples in 6.56 are, for the purposes of the simplified and streamlined approach, of an illustrative nature, and any conclusion that such contributions are unique and valuable should be based on the accurate delineation of the qualifying transaction. Based on the examples provided in 6.56, contributions that may be unique and valuable in the context of qualifying transactions may include the design and control of marketing programmes, the direction of and establishing priorities for creative undertakings relating to the marketing of the products distributed, the control over strategic decisions regarding development programmes for marketing intangibles, or the management and control of associated budgets. Other relevant contributions may also include important decisions regarding the defence and protection of marketing intangibles, such as trademarks or trade names, and important decisions regarding ongoing quality control over functions performed by independent or associated enterprises that may have a material effect on the value of the marketing intangible under consideration.

effect of restricting the number of competitors in the market. In assessing the impact of contributions made to obtain the license, it is important to consider the contributions of both the distributor and other group members in supplying the capabilities necessary to obtain the license. Chapter VI, Section B, including paragraph 6.34, should be considered and applied in assessing these functions and whether they constitute a unique and valuable contribution.

3.3.2. Scoping criterion 13.b – quantitative filter

22. After the application of scoping criterion 13.a, scoping criterion 13.b acts to exclude qualifying transactions from the scope of the simplified and streamlined approach using quantitative filters.

23. These quantitative filters provide a simplified mechanism for the assessment of whether a tested party is in scope, in conjunction with the other scoping criteria.[22] The upper bound, for example, acts as a proxy to exclude qualifying transactions from scope where the ratio of operating expenses to sales might indicate that additional functions are performed, suggesting that the pricing methodology of Section 5 of this guidance would have reduced reliability in practice. Consequently, the quantitative filter is applied so that the pricing methodology of Section 5 of this guidance may reliably be applied to establish arm's length prices for qualifying transactions.

Calculating the quantitative filters in 13.b

24. Given that the values of both operating expenses and net revenues will vary over time, this will inevitably entail certain distributors moving in and out of scope. In order to make qualification for scope more consistent, the calculation of the ratio provided above should be based on a three-year weighted average. The three-year weighted average ratio should be calculated on a year-on-year basis for the purposes of determining whether a qualifying transaction is in-scope. For example, for a qualifying transaction in fiscal year *x*, the three-year weighted average ratio would be derived by (A) taking the sum of the annual operating expenses for years *x-3*, *x-2*, and *x-1*, then (B) taking the sum of the annual net revenues over the same period, and then dividing (A) by (B) to derive the appropriate percentage.[23] [24]

---

[22] Quantitative scoping filters are used in the context of the simplified and streamlined approach as a simplification measure and do not provide any definitive indication of what functions are performed or the characterisation for distributors that fall out of scope or in general. Where a distributor falls out of scope, this should not be taken as implying any arm's length price for the controlled transaction, regardless of the scoping criteria used. For the avoidance of doubt, a determination of arm's length prices in such circumstances should follow the principles articulated in the remainder of these Guidelines. The quantitative filters applied to determine whether a qualifying transaction is within the scope of the simplified and streamlined approach are only used for that purpose, and not, for example, replicated in the pricing methodology used to establish returns for in-scope distributors.

[23] When a distributor performs non-distribution activities, and where that distributor remains in scope after applying scoping criterion 14.b, then the ratios described under 13.b should be calculated based on the relevant allocation or apportionment of revenues and operating expenses to the distribution activity only.

[24] In calculating each ratio, it is important to determine what are the appropriate operating expenses and what are the appropriate net revenues that should be accounted for. This determination should be made based on an accurate delineation of the transaction and by applying the principles articulated in Chapter II of these Guidelines. Paragraphs 2.99 and 2.100 of these Guidelines may provide some relevant input to making the determination of the appropriate treatment of operating expenses. Moreover, paragraphs 2.96 and 2.97 of these Guidelines provide some relevant input to making the determination of the appropriate treatment of revenues, rebates, and discounts. The treatment of pass-through expenses should be evaluated in calculating the ratio. Under an accurate delineation of the transaction, there may be circumstances where pass-through costs are delineated and should not be taken into account when calculating the ratio. Such a determination should be made in light of the general principles articulated elsewhere in

Where the qualifying transaction has been in place for two years, a two-year weighted average ratio should be used, and where the qualifying transaction has been in place for only one year the ratio should be calculated based on the financial results for that year.

3.3.3. Scoping criterion 14.a – Non-tangible goods and services exclusion and commodities exclusion

Non-tangible goods and services

25. The simplified and streamlined approach applies to tangible goods and does not capture the distribution and marketing of non-tangible goods or services. The simplified and streamlined approach applies to qualifying transactions involving the distribution of tangible goods for which there is broad consistency in the overall supply chain and functional analysis.

Commodities

26. Qualifying transactions involving the trading, marketing or distribution of commodities are excluded from scope. This sub-section articulates the breadth of the exemption and defines the relevant commodities, both using a general principle and listing some specific commodities as examples.

27. The general principle is that the exclusion is broad in nature and encompasses transactions involving the trading, marketing, or distribution of products of a commodity nature, whether or not they have a quoted price, and includes transactions where the commodity has undergone qualifying processing. For the purposes of the simplified and streamlined approach, a commodity may be any of the following:

a. A renewable or non-renewable physical product that is primarily derived from the earth's crust, land or water. These renewable or non-renewable physical products can be manifested in a solid, liquid or gas state and take various forms such as a hydrocarbon, mineral, mineraloid and agricultural product.

c. A renewable or non-renewable physical product that has undergone qualifying processing.

d. A product that is in accordance with the definition of a commodity provided for in paragraph 2.18 of these Guidelines.

28. The definitions of a hydrocarbon, mineral, mineraloid and agricultural commodity are:

a. Hydrocarbon means any organic compound consisting predominantly of carbon and hydrogen molecules that is in solid, liquid or gaseous form occurring naturally in or on the earth or in the seabed or sub-soil and which was formed by or subjected to a geological process and includes but not limited to crude oil, oil sands, heavy oils and natural gas occurring in a subsurface oil and gas reservoir, deposit, or in a stockpile.

b. Mineral means any inorganic substance that exhibits crystalline characteristics, in solid form, occurring naturally in or on the earth's crust or in or under water and which was formed by or subjected to a geological process, and includes but not limited to clay, gems, gravel, metal, ore, rock, sand, soil, stone, salt and any such substance occurring in an ore body, ore deposit, or in a stockpile or tailings.

c. Mineraloid means any substance that does not exhibit crystalline characteristics whether in solid, liquid, or gaseous form, occurring naturally in or on the earth or in or under water and which was

---

these Guidelines and the facts and circumstances. Moreover, it should be noted that reference to paragraphs 2.96, 2.97, 2.99 and 2.100 of these Guidelines should not be interpreted as modifying existing guidance concerning the most appropriate methods that may be appropriate to evaluate arm's length remuneration of distributors.

formed by or subjected to a geological process, and includes but is not limited to amber, coal, obsidian and opals, and any such substance occurring in an ore body, ore deposit, or in a stockpile or tailings.

d. Agricultural means any primary product, raw or processed, that is marketed for consumption and includes but is not limited to animal biproducts such as dairy or fibre, livestock, grains, coffee, tea, fishery, forestry, fruit, and vegetables.

29. The term "qualifying processing" means processing undertaken to bond, concentrate, isolate, purify, refine, blend, separate, raise, harvest, produce or liberate a hydrocarbon, mineral, mineraloids or agricultural product. It includes the processing undertaken to produce all intermediate products obtained from a hydrocarbon, mineral, mineraloids or agricultural product up to and including the following non-exhaustive list of products:

- liquefied natural gas, liquefied petroleum gas and other natural gas liquids, diesel, kerosene, gasoline, and hydrogen.
- metal oxides, metal hydroxides, anodes, cathodes, cast metals, aluminium, and alloys.
- cattle, poultry, swine, sheep, goat, wheat, milk powder, cotton, maize, barley, rice, soybeans, cocoa, corn.

30. To provide additional clarity to the commodity product-based exclusion, a non-exhaustive list of examples of excluded commodities is provided here. Common examples of metals include aluminium, copper, nickel, iron, tin, gold, lead, platinum group metals, silver, manganese, cobalt, molybdenum, lithium carbonate/hydroxide, boric acid, titanium, uranium, and zinc, as well as metal oxides and metal hydroxides. Examples of an anode include copper and graphite anodes. Examples of cathodes are copper, cobalt and nickel cathodes. Common examples of oil and gas products include crude oil, oil sands, heavy oils, natural gas, naphtha, liquefied natural gas, liquefied petroleum gas and other natural gas liquids, diesel, kerosene, gasoline, and hydrogen. Common examples of agricultural products include livestock such as cattle, poultry, swine, sheep, goats, soft commodities such as wheat, cotton, maize, oats, barley, rice, soybeans, cocoa sugar, corn, coffee, and fishery, forestry, fruit, and vegetables.

31. The products listed are typically in the final step of the production process and it is possible that an MNE Group could also sell products that are in an earlier form to this stage i.e. intermediate products. To the extent that intermediate products fulfil the earlier definitions, they would still be captured under the commodity product-based exclusion.

3.3.4. Scoping criterion 14. b - Non-distribution activities separate from the qualifying transaction

32. Distributors that engage in qualifying transactions sometimes engage in non-distribution activities. Where such a tested party performs non-distribution activities, the qualifying transaction may only remain in scope where, based on an accurate delineation of the transaction, it can be adequately evaluated on a separate basis to any non-distribution transactions, and it can be reliably priced separately from any non-distribution transactions under the principles of paragraphs 3.9 – 3.12 of these Guidelines. Illustrations of the application of paragraphs 3.9 – 3.12 in the context of the simplified and streamlined approach are provided in paragraphs 35 to 37.

33. Examples of non-distribution activities include manufacturing, research and development, procurement, financing, or retail distribution performed above the de minimis threshold considered in the Definitions to this guidance. Objective measurements might be used to determine whether the distributor performs these activities. For example,

- for manufacturing, the existence of manufacturing inventory (direct labour and/or work-in-process inventory) and/or the existence of manufacturing assets (e.g., property, plant, equipment);

- for research and development, the incurrence of research and development expenses, even if reimbursed;
- for procurement, the existence of procurement commission income;
- for financing, the existence of loan assets on the balance sheet; and
- for retail, the sales profile of the distributor (for example, evidence of the sales channels of the distributor and extent of sales made to retail customers), or the holding or leasing of retail storefront property.

34. A tested party may undertake a combination of distribution and non-distribution activities for which it does not establish separate prices, and in practice treats these activities as a bundled transaction. For example, a distributor of products might also provide services that are separate to the distribution transaction, but where it only charges one price for the combined supply of products and services as a bundled transaction. Given that these separate (in this case, distribution and services) activities are not separately transacted for with related or unrelated parties and priced at arm's length, the distribution activity might not be able to be adequately evaluated separately or reliably priced separately, given the absence of separate revenue streams for the bundled transaction. Examples of situations where adequate separate evaluation and reliable separate pricing may be challenging are provided in the subsequent sub-section.

Illustrations of where evaluation of the distribution transaction on a separate basis may be inadequate, or pricing on a separate basis may be unreliable

35. Paragraphs 3.9 – 3.12 of these Guidelines provide examples where transactions are so closely linked or continuous such that they cannot be adequately evaluated on a separate basis. Some examples applied to the context of the simplified and streamlined approach are provided below.

36. Assume that a distributor contributes to the development of manufacturing patents for products that are unrelated to the products distributed. The qualifying transaction would remain in scope provided that the revenues, direct and indirect costs, and assets relevant to the development of the patents can be reliably separated, whether they are attributed or apportioned, from the qualifying transaction so that any remaining revenues, direct and indirect costs, or assets are relevant only to the qualifying distribution transaction.

37. One further example of where both adequate separate evaluation and reliable separate pricing is challenging is where an MNE group bundles the provision of goods and services, where it may be difficult to unbundle these activities and consequently quantify the revenue and profits attributable to each activity. One example of this is where a distributor provides consumer financing (for example, materially deferred payment terms or financing directly related to the sales of products) alongside the sale of tangible goods. In such situations, separating out the financial results relating to the distribution of tangible goods from the financing could be challenging.[25]

[25] Per Section D.8 of Chapter I, and paragraph 1.179, of these Guidelines, MNE group synergies may arise in the context of controlled transactions, for which specific compensation at arm's length may be justified. These principles are also relevant to consider in this simplified and streamlined approach. For example, where a distributor makes contributions to create such MNE group synergies, or where a non-distribution economic activity undertaken within the same MNE as the distributor leads to similar contributions being made that benefit the distributor, this may lead to challenges in the adequate separate evaluation of the qualifying transaction, on the basis that compensation may need to be imputed with respect to the creation of the synergy.

Guidance relating to the practical allocation of revenues, costs, assets, and liabilities to the distribution activities.

38. Paragraphs 2.83, 2.84, 2.85, 2.86, 2.91 and 2.98, and Sections B.2.2.2 and B.2.3 of Chapter VII provide for the general principles relating to the allocation of revenues, costs, assets, and liabilities with respect to a distribution transaction and other transactions. An allocation of assets for the purposes of pricing the in scope qualifying transaction should follow this guidance and the underlying principles, even where assets may not be specifically mentioned in the guidance.

39. Tax administrations will require various information to assess the reliability of the allocation or apportionment of revenues, costs, assets, and liabilities, and taxpayers should prepare that information under the documentation requirements considered in Section 6. In particular, tax administrations may need to evaluate internal financial reporting, the organisation chart of the entity and the management structure of the entity, over several fiscal years. Tax administrations may also need to review whether the allocation or apportionment of revenues, costs, assets, and liabilities has been performed consistently.

4 Application of the most appropriate method principle to in-scope transactions

40. The selection of a transfer pricing method always aims at finding the most appropriate method for a particular case. However, in evaluating the choice of method for in-scope transactions, it is neither necessary to prove that a particular method is *not* suitable under the circumstances, nor is it necessary that *all* transfer pricing methods should be analysed in depth or tested in each case in selecting the most appropriate method.[26]

41. Based on the economically relevant characteristics of in-scope transactions and the information available on comparable uncontrolled transactions, the transactional net margin method is chosen as the most appropriate method under the simplified and streamlined approach.

42. However, it is recognised that there may be instances (although these may be rare, as the distribution of commodities is excluded from scope) where the application of the comparable uncontrolled price method using internal comparables could be potentially more appropriate to apply to price in-scope transactions. For those instances, for transactions within the scope of the simplified and streamlined approach, an exception is provided that allows that the comparable uncontrolled price method using internal comparables can be used to reliably price in-scope transactions where that is in accordance with Part II B of Chapter II and A.4.2. of Chapter III of these Guidelines and both the comparables and any information utilised to determine that the application of the comparable uncontrolled price method is more appropriate are readily available to tax administrations and taxpayers.

[26] See paragraphs 2.2, 2.8 of these Guidelines.

5 Determining the return under the simplified and streamlined approach

43. The methodology and guidance included throughout Section 5, including the design elements described in 5.1, 5.2 and 5.3, and the defined terms relied upon in these elements, are specific to the application of the simplified and streamlined approach. As with all other design elements of the simplified and streamlined approach, neither the inclusion of the operating expense cross-check, nor the data availability mechanism, nor any individual features within those design elements should be construed as implying that they would be included in the application of a most appropriate method determined under the remainder of these Guidelines for any transaction.

5.1. Pricing matrix

44. Application of the relevant benchmarking search criteria as well as additional screening and manual review to reflect the scoping criteria has led to the development of a global dataset of companies involved in baseline marketing and distribution activities. The financial information derived from that global dataset has in part formed the basis for the approximation of arm's length results which has been translated into a pricing matrix.[27]

45. The approximation of arm's length results has been presented as matrix segments according to the following factors: net operating asset intensity (OAS), operating expense intensity (OES) and industry groupings.

46. For the purposes of the simplified and streamlined approach, return on sales has been applied as the net profit indicator for the purpose of establishing pricing outcomes for in-scope transactions.

[27] See Appendix A for further details.

Table 5.1. Pricing Matrix (return on sales %) derived from the global dataset

Industry Grouping Factor Intensity	Industry Grouping 1	Industry Grouping 2	Industry Grouping 3
(A) OAS 45% or more, any level of OES	**3.50%**	**5.00%**	**5.50%**
(B) OAS 30% to less than 45%, any level of OES	**3.00%**	**3.75%**	**4.50%**
(C) OAS 15% to less than 30%, any level of OES	**2.50%**	**3.00%**	**4.50%**
(D) OAS less than 15%, OES 10% or more	**1.75%**	**2.00%**	**3.00%**
(E) OAS less than 15%, OES less than 10%	**1.50%**	**1.75%**	**2.25%**

47. In order to determine the return for a tested party involved in in-scope transactions for the relevant fiscal year, a tax administration and relevant taxpayer[28] will apply the following 3-step process:

a. Step 1 - determine the relevant industry grouping(s) of the tested party from the three possible groupings (i.e. industry grouping 1, 2, 3) and identify the applicable vertical column(s) of return on sales in the pricing matrix in table 5.1 that correspond to that industry grouping. In the case that the products distributed fall into more than one industry grouping, the proportion of sales falling into each industry grouping should be calculated. In the case that at least 80% of sales fall into a single industry grouping and so 20% of sales or less fall into different industry grouping(s), the latter will not be determinative for setting the matrix return and instead the return will be set by reference only to the relevant matrix cell for the industry grouping where the majority of sales fall. In the case that more than 20% of sales are from products which fall into a second and/or third industry grouping, a weighted average return should be calculated.
b. Step 2 - determine the relevant factor intensity classification of the tested party[29] from the five possible classifications (i.e. factor intensity classification A, B, C, D, and E) and identify the applicable horizontal row of return on sales in the pricing matrix in table 5.1 that correspond to that factor intensity classification. The factor intensity classification of the tested party should be calculated based on a weighted average of the three preceding fiscal years.[30]
c. Step 3 - identify the range from the pricing matrix segment that corresponds to the intersection of the industry grouping(s) and the factor intensity classification of the tested party. If needed, the weighted average return should be calculated by multiplying each return from the relevant cells of the matrix by the proportion of sales to be priced by reference to that cell and totalling these proportional returns to give a single weighted average return rate applicable to all sales by that

[28] With reference to the implementation options outlined in paragraph 7 of this guidance, "relevant taxpayer" refers to: (i) taxpayers who elect to apply the simplified and streamlined approach in a jurisdiction of residence that permits such election, and (ii) taxpayers who are otherwise obligated to apply the simplified and streamlined approach in the jurisdiction of residence.

[29] For the purpose of calculating the net operating assets of the tested party for relevant years and mitigating the risk of distortive credit terms, an accounts payable days guardrail of 90 days applies, such that the value of creditors used in the respective calculations shall not exceed cost of goods sold / 365 * 90. An illustrative example, example 6, on the practical application of the accounts payable days guardrail is included in Appendix B.

[30] Where the qualifying transaction has been in place for two years, a two-year weighted average ratio should be used, and where the qualifying transaction has been in place for only one year the ratio should be calculated based on the financial results for that year.

distributor. In this way, the weighting of factor intensity classifications relies only on the proportion of sales assigned to each industry grouping and does not require a calculation that recognises the operating expenses and assets that are specific to each industry grouping.

48. The return derived from application of step 3 in Section 5.1 will produce a range equal to the return on sales percentage[31] derived from the pricing matrix (Table 5.1) plus or minus 0.5%. Any point within that acceptable range can be relied upon for the purpose of demonstrating compliance with Section 5.1 and will form the basis for any subsequent adjustments that may apply in accordance with Section 5.2 and 5.3 below.

49. For the purposes of the simplified and streamlined approach, relevant taxpayers will apply and test the actual outcome of in-scope transactions to demonstrate the conditions of these transactions were consistent with the simplified and streamlined approach on an *ex post* basis (i.e. the arm's length outcome-testing approach). Such test typically takes place as part of the process for establishing the tax return at year-end.[32]

50. In asserting the application of the simplified and streamlined approach to in-scope transactions, tax administrations should bear in mind the guidance in paragraph 3.60 of these Guidelines regarding controlled transactions that are within the range. Moreover, when the margin reported by a relevant taxpayer falls outside the range resulting from the appropriate application of the simplified and streamlined approach by a tax administration, tax administrations should use the return on sales percentage derived from the pricing matrix (table 5.1) to adjust the margin of the controlled transaction.

5.2. Operating expense cross-check

51. For the purposes of the simplified and streamlined approach, an operating expense cross-check is applied as a guardrail within which the primary return on sales net profit indicator is applied. Where the application of the return on sales net profit indicator produces a result outside of the pre-defined operating expense cap-and-collar range specified in table 5.2 below, the profitability of the tested party will be adjusted in accordance with paragraph 52(d).

[31] In the case where more than 20% of sales are from products which fall outside of a single industry grouping, the return derived from step 3 will produce a range equal to the weighted average return determined in accordance with paragraph 47 plus or minus 0.5%.

[32] See paragraph 3.70 of these Guidelines.

Table 5.2. Operating expense cap-and-collar range

	Operating expense cap-and-collar range		
Factor intensity	Default cap rates	Alternative cap rates for qualifying jurisdictions	Collar rate
High OAS (A)	70%	80%	10%
Medium OAS (B+C)	60%	70%	
Low OAS (D+E)	40%	45%	

52. The operating expense cross-check applies to all in-scope transactions and requires a tax administration and relevant taxpayer to apply the following 4-step process:

a. Step 1 - a tax administration and taxpayer will determine the return on sales for the tested party in accordance with the guidance in Section 5.1 and compute an equivalent return on operating expense derived from that return.
b. Step 2 – the tax administration and taxpayer will determine the applicable operating expense cap-and-collar range derived from table 5.2. The applicable cap rate is determined by reference to: (i) the factor intensity classification of the tested party[33], and (ii) whether the tested party is subject to the default cap rates[34] or alternative cap rates[35] for qualifying jurisdictions within the meaning of Section 5.2.
c. Step 3 - the tax administration and taxpayer will compare the equivalent return on operating expense of the tested party against the operating expense cap-and-collar determined in Step 2.
d. Step 4 - where the equivalent return on operating expense of the tested party determined in Step 1 falls within the operating expense cap-and-collar range, no further adjustment is required to the return on sales calculated in Section 5.1. However, where the equivalent return on operating expense of the tested party determined in Step 1 exceeds the operating expense cap, the return on sales of the tested party will be adjusted downwards until it results in an equivalent return on operating expense equal to the operating expense cap. Conversely, where the equivalent return on operating expense of the tested party falls below the operating expense collar, the return on sales of the tested party will be adjusted upwards until it results in an equivalent return on operating expense equal to the operating expense collar.

5.3. Data availability mechanism for qualifying jurisdictions

53. The data availability mechanism is intended to account for cases where there is no or insufficient data in the global dataset for a particular tested party jurisdiction and that jurisdiction is a qualifying jurisdiction within the meaning of Section 5.3.[36]

---

[33] This should correspond to the factor intensity classification of the tested party as determined in accordance with paragraph 47(b) in Section 5.1.

[34] Default cap rates apply for the purpose of step 2 unless the tested party is located in a qualifying jurisdiction within the meaning of Section 5.2.

[35] Alternative cap rates apply for the purpose of step 2 where the tested party is located in a qualifying jurisdiction within the meaning of Section 5.2.

[36] See paragraph 1.167 of these Guidelines.

54. Where a tested party is located in a qualifying jurisdiction, an adjustment will be made to the return initially determined under Section 5.1 and Section 5.2 where applicable. A relevant taxpayer in an aforementioned qualifying jurisdiction will earn an adjusted return in accordance with the following formula:

$$\text{Adjusted return on sales} = ROS^{TP} + (NRA^{J} \times OAS^{TP})$$

Where –

- ROS^{TP} is the return on sales percentage of the tested party calculated in accordance with Section 5.1 and Section 5.2 where applicable.
- NRA^{J} is the net risk adjustment percentage of the qualifying jurisdiction derived from table 5.3 below, where the applicable category is determined by reference to the sovereign credit rating[37] of the qualifying jurisdiction of the tested party applicable on the first day of the relevant fiscal year.[38]
- OAS^{TP} is the net operating asset intensity percentage of the tested party for the relevant fiscal year but will not exceed 85% for the purpose of computing the adjusted return on sales of the tested party.

---

[37] Where there exists multiple and varying sovereign credit ratings for a qualifying jurisdiction from the recognised independent ratings agencies, the determination of the applicable net risk adjustment percentage from table 5.3 should be based on the sovereign credit rating for that qualifying jurisdiction that was issued or re-affirmed nearest to the first day of the relevant fiscal year.

[38] Where there exists no sovereign credit rating for a qualifying jurisdiction from the recognised independent ratings agencies, the applicable net risk adjustment percentage will equal the average net risk adjustment percentage for all non-investment grades derived from table 5.3.

Table 5.3. Net risk adjustment percentage to be applied to the OAS of a Tested Party in qualifying jurisdictions

Sovereign Credit Rating Category		Net risk adjustment %[39]
Investment grade	BBB+	0.0%
	BBB	0.0%
	BBB-	0.3%
Non-investment grade	BB+	0.7%
	BB	1.2%
	BB-	1.8%
	B+	2.8%
	B	3.8%
	B-	4.9%
	CCC+	5.9%
	CCC	7.5%
	CCC- (or lower)	8.6%

5.4. Periodic updates

55. In order to simplify compliance burdens associated with administering the simplified and streamlined approach, the analysis supporting the determination of the ranges referenced in Section 5.1 and operating expense cap-and-collar rates in Section 5.2 will be updated every five years unless there is a significant change in market conditions that warrants an interim update.

56. The financial data and other datapoints referenced in Section 5.1 and Section 5.3 will be reviewed annually and updated where necessary.

[39] The methodology applied to calculate the net risk adjustment percentages in this table comprises determining the five-year average sovereign debt default spread for each credit rating grade (sourced from data compiled by Aswath Damodaran, NYU Stern School of Business) less a double counting adjustment that seeks to approximate for the existing country risk present in the global dataset.

6 Documentation

57. In general, transfer pricing documentation ensures that tax administrations have access to the necessary information to conduct risk assessment processes and/or to audit the taxpayer's transfer pricing practices[40]. In the case of the simplified and streamlined approach, documentation is important to ensure that tax administrations have sufficient and reliable information to assess whether taxpayers' qualifying transactions meet the scoping criteria and taxpayers have properly applied the simplified and streamlined approach to in-scope transactions.

58. This section identifies the main items of information in the local file that can be useful in substantiating the taxpayer's position on the applicability of the simplified and streamlined approach and provide tax administrations with the relevant information for its application. When considering the introduction of targeted documentation requirements for the simplified and streamlined approach, jurisdictions may consider simplifying such requirements for small and medium enterprises to limit their costs and compliance burden.[41]

59. The three-tiered approach to transfer pricing documentation described in Chapter V includes a local file, which provides detailed information on the taxpayer's specific intercompany transactions. The documentation approach for the simplified and streamlined approach is built on the premise that the current content of the local file (see Annex II of Chapter V) includes the items of information and documents which are relevant to examine the taxpayer's position.

60. The following items of information may already be included in the local file and can be particularly relevant and useful to tax administrations in assessing whether the taxpayer's qualifying transactions meet the scoping criteria, and, if the taxpayer applied the pricing methodology, whether it did so properly:

a. An explanation on the delineation of the in-scope qualifying transaction, including the functional analysis of the taxpayer and relevant associated enterprises with respect to the in-scope transactions, and the context in which such transactions take place (e.g. whether there are any other commercial or financial relations between the tested party/taxpayer and other associated enterprises that may influence the accurate delineation of the qualifying transaction potentially in scope).

b. Written contract or agreements concluded governing the qualifying transaction and supporting the explanation on the delineation of the in-scope qualifying transaction described in (a).

c. Calculations showing the determination of the relevant revenue, costs and assets allocated or attributed to the in-scope transaction;

d. Information and allocation schedules showing how the financial data used in assessing the applicability of the simplified and streamlined approach and applying the transfer pricing method ties to the annual financial statements.

[40] See paragraphs 5.5 and 5.6 of these Guidelines.

[41] See paragraph 5.33 of these Guidelines.

61. In relation to the information item in 60(b), where it is consistent with the scoping criteria and the conduct of the parties, the provision of a written contract would ease the administration of the simplified and streamlined approach when a taxpayer is seeking to apply the approach to a qualifying transaction. However, regardless of whether a written contract is in place, tax administrations or taxpayers can assert or challenge the approach based on the accurate delineation of the transaction performed under the principles articulated in Chapter I of these Guidelines.[42]

62. Financial information on the tested party is needed to understand whether the qualifying transaction meets the scoping criteria, irrespective of whether the tested party is a domestic or foreign entity.[43] Accordingly, the taxpayer will also need to provide the annual financial accounts of the tested party for the relevant fiscal years.

63. Where one or more items of information relevant to assess the application of the simplified and streamlined approach are not included as part of the transfer pricing documentation, tax administrations may require taxpayers to provide them upon request. Importantly, making this information available to tax administrations as part of the annual transfer pricing requirements or upon request may translate into fewer follow-up requests for information and audits for the taxpayer, as well as in a more efficient use of tax administrations' resources.

64. In addition to the information in the local file, taxpayers and tax administrations should leverage the information provided in the master file to support their position with regards to the application of the pricing approach. In particular, the master file can provide valuable information on the MNE Group's business, such as main products, main geographic markets, pricing policy or the general strategy of the MNE Group for the development, ownership and exploitation of intangibles. As a matter of good practice, to avoid excessive compliance burden for taxpayers, when evaluating the applicability of the simplified and streamlined approach to qualifying transactions of a given taxpayers, tax administrations should refrain from requesting the taxpayer to produce or submit information already in the hands of the tax administration.

65. The fact that the taxpayer has prepared and submitted the above information to the tax administration does not prevent the tax administration from examining the taxpayer's self-assessment on whether the scoping criteria are met and the pricing methodology has been applied properly.

66. Finally, when the taxpayer is seeking to apply the simplified and streamlined approach for the first time, the taxpayer should include in its local file, or in any other documentation relevant to the application of the approach, a consent to apply the approach for a minimum of 3 years, unless transactions are no longer in scope during that period, or there is a significant change in the taxpayer's business, and notify that circumstance to the tax authorities of the jurisdictions involved in the qualifying transaction. As part of the first-time notification procedure, tax administrations could require the taxpayer to provide some or all of the items of information listed in paragraph 60. In addition, tax administrations may require taxpayers seeking to apply the simplified and streamlined approach to provide a written contract signed prior to the occurrence of the qualifying transaction. The preceding sentence is not intended to change in any way the role of a written contract in the accurate delineation of the transaction, as discussed in Section D.1 of Chapter I.

---

[42] See paragraph 1.49 of these Guidelines.

[43] See paragraph 3.22 of these Guidelines.

7 Transitional issues

67. MNE Groups may reorganise their distribution business models and, as result, conclude qualifying transactions that meet the conditions to be in-scope of the simplified and streamlined approach. Equally, there may be MNE Groups with in-scope transactions which, following the restructure of their distribution arrangements, no longer meet the conditions to apply the simplified and streamlined approach.

68. As stated in paragraph 9.34, MNE Groups are free to organise their business operations as they see fit and tax administrations do not have the right to dictate to MNE Groups how to design their structure or where to locate their business operations. Tax administrations, however, have the right to determine the tax consequences resulting from the reorganisation. In this regard, the guidance in Chapter IX remains relevant whether the simplified and streamlined approach is applicable to the pre-restructuring or post-restructuring qualifying transactions.

69. Some Associated Enterprises may attempt to artificially reorganise their arrangements to derive tax advantages from the application of the simplified and streamlined approach. Such scenarios may come under greater scrutiny by tax authorities to prevent the use of the approach for tax planning opportunities and jurisdictions may adopt targeted approaches to address these concerns.[44]

70. In some instances, the simplified and streamlined approach may apply to a restructured distributor with built-in losses from prior fiscal years. The tax treatment of such losses, in particular whether they are available or can be deductible, depends on each jurisdiction's domestic legislation and administrative procedures and is not within the scope of this guidance.

[44] Any business restructuring should be properly documented in the master file and the local file. See paragraphs 9.32 - 9.33 of these Guidelines.

8 Tax certainty and elimination of double taxation

71. Where a tax administration makes a primary adjustment resulting in double taxation of the profits derived from the relevant qualifying transaction, a corresponding adjustment can mitigate or eliminate double taxation by adjusting downwards the tax liability of the associated enterprise in a second tax jurisdiction. Some jurisdictions may be able to remedy economic double taxation through unilateral corresponding adjustments making use of provisions in their domestic laws.[45] However, most jurisdictions would only be able to consider corresponding adjustments as part of a Mutual Agreement Procedure.[46]

72. Taxpayers, on filing for a Mutual Agreement Procedure, where one or more of the jurisdictions relevant to the Mutual Agreement Procedure has not chosen to apply or accept the simplified and streamlined approach, should base any justification of their position[47] only on the remainder of these Guidelines.[48] In a Mutual Agreement Procedure or resulting arbitration procedure, where one or more of the jurisdictions relevant to the Mutual Agreement Procedure has not chosen to apply or accept the simplified and streamlined approach, then the competent authorities of both jurisdictions engaged in that Mutual Agreement Procedure must justify their positions based only on the remainder of these Guidelines. Specifically in such cases, the simplified and streamlined approach under this guidance must not be considered or referenced by the relevant competent authorities as an approach which is treated as leading to an acceptable outcome.[49] This includes for the purposes of conducting the Mutual Agreement Procedure, as a basis of a resolution of the Mutual Agreement Procedure, or by any party (including arbitrators) in the conduct of any arbitration procedure.[50]

---

[45] See Commentary to Article 25, para. 12.

[46] See paragraph 4.32 of these Guidelines.

[47] This specifically refers to situations where a taxpayer should present a position to a competent authority when filing for a Mutual Agreement Procedure or chooses to present such a position and is not to suggest that a taxpayer is obligated to present a position in order to access a Mutual Agreement Procedure. In other words, a taxpayer that does not justify its position only on the remainder of the Guidelines still has access to a Mutual Agreement Procedure.

[48] If there is a competent authority agreement that calls for application of the simplified and streamlined approach, or if the jurisdictions of both parties that take part in the transaction elect to apply the simplified and streamlined approach in the relevant case, then the competent authorities will rely on the simplified and streamlined approach. In such circumstances, taxpayers can also rely on such approach. If there is no such competent authority agreement, and if the competent authorities have not otherwise agreed to apply the simplified and streamlined approach in the relevant case, then, in the event that the taxpayer presents a position, it should be based on the remainder of these Guidelines.

[49] See footnote 54.

[50] Note that the same principles apply to unilateral corresponding adjustments described in paragraph 71, which are provided under the domestic law of the jurisdictions where such procedures are legally permissible, based on the domestic law of such jurisdictions.

73. This general principle is illustrated below, considering two potential sources of double taxation. These scenarios should not be considered as being exhaustive, and instead should be considered as an attempt to illustrate the process by which such double taxation may be relieved.

74. One potential source of double taxation could occur where the simplified and streamlined approach has been applied by a taxpayer to price an in-scope transaction in a jurisdiction that has chosen to apply the approach, and a primary adjustment is made by the counterparty jurisdiction based on the remainder of these Guidelines.

75. To remedy any resulting double taxation, a request for a corresponding adjustment should be analysed under paragraph 2 of Article 9. Since the primary adjustment is made by a jurisdiction based on the remainder of the Guidelines, this request could be made to the jurisdiction where the simplified and streamlined approach applies.[51] In such a case, to the extent the primary adjustment can be substantiated under the remainder of these Guidelines,[52] the competent authority of the jurisdiction where the simplified and streamlined approach applies shall provide relief from double taxation by making a corresponding adjustment.

76. If relief from double taxation cannot be achieved in that manner under paragraph 2 of Article 9,[53] this may lead to a Mutual Agreement Procedure. In these cases, taxpayers engaged in a Mutual Agreement Procedure should support their position only based on the remainder of these Guidelines.

77. In such cases, where one of the jurisdictions in the Mutual Agreement Procedure is a jurisdiction that has chosen not to apply the simplified and streamlined approach, the simplified and streamlined approach under this guidance should not be considered or referenced by the competent authorities as an approach which leads to a result which is treated as an acceptable outcome for purposes of the Mutual Agreement Procedure or any arbitration procedure.[54] This includes for the purposes of conducting the Mutual Agreement Procedure, as a basis of a resolution of the Mutual Agreement Procedure, or by any party (including arbitrators) in the conduct of any arbitration procedure. In such situations the competent authority of the tax administration originally applying or accepting the application of the simplified and streamlined approach must justify its position in the Mutual Agreement Procedure and any resulting arbitration procedure based on the remainder of these Guidelines.

78. Another potential source of double taxation could occur where the simplified and streamlined approach is applied under the second option discussed in paragraph 7 and a primary adjustment is made by a tax administration to ensure that taxation is levied in accordance with the outcome of applying the simplified and streamlined approach. In such cases a request for relief from double taxation may be made to the counterparty jurisdiction under a Mutual Agreement Procedure. The relevant competent authorities should note the guidance in paragraphs 4.117 and 4.131 of these Guidelines in attempting to relieve double taxation. Where the counterparty jurisdiction has not agreed to apply the simplified and streamlined approach in a competent authority agreement with the jurisdiction making the adjustment, or to apply it specifically to resolve double taxation in the case under consideration,[55] the competent authority of the jurisdiction where the adjustment was made must substantiate its position based on the remainder of these

---

[51] Depending on the applicable tax treaty, a taxpayer may be required to file for the Mutual Agreement Procedure in its jurisdiction of residence.

[52] See paragraph 6 of the commentary to Article 9(2) of the Model Tax Convention.

[53] Equally considering the same commentary in paragraph 6 of Article 9(2) of the Model Tax Convention.

[54] However, the outcome of applying the simplified and streamlined approach may in some cases be consistent with the outcome of applying the remainder of these Guidelines.

[55] See paragraph 79.

Guidelines in any Mutual Agreement Procedure or resulting arbitration, noting the general principles articulated in paragraph 72 above.

79. Whether or not it applies the simplified and streamlined approach, a jurisdiction may provide a corresponding adjustment that reflects the outcome of the simplified and streamlined approach on a case-by-case basis if it considers that it produces an acceptable outcome in a specific case.[56] Jurisdictions may also choose to enter into competent authority agreements with other jurisdictions to provide corresponding adjustments according to the result determined by applying the simplified and streamlined approach. It is recommended that in such an agreement, the jurisdiction considering the corresponding adjustment has the ability to verify whether the qualifying transaction meets the conditions to apply the approach and whether the approach has been applied correctly in determining the amount of the primary adjustment.[57]

80. For the avoidance of doubt, for any agreement reached under Article 25 of the Model Tax Convention (including bilateral or multilateral APA cases as well as Mutual Agreement Procedure cases)[58] obtained prior to the implementation of the simplified and streamlined approach, the terms and conditions of such agreements would continue to be valid in relation to the covered qualifying transactions. This approach respects legally binding agreements and avoids uncertainty as to whether disputes already settled between competent authorities may be subject to review and reassessment and enhances predictability for concerned taxpayers.

---

[56] If the jurisdictions of both parties that take part in the transaction elect to apply the simplified and streamlined approach, these jurisdictions would be expected to accept the outcome determined by applying the simplified and streamlined approach to the in-scope transaction and provide reciprocal corresponding adjustments or accept the result as an outcome in a Mutual Agreement Procedure accordingly.

[57] See guidance in paragraphs 5 and 6 of the Commentary on Article 9 and Section C.2 of Chapter IV of these Guidelines.

[58] In the case of unilateral APAs reached prior to the adoption of the streamlined and simplified approach, this approach respects legally binding agreements between a jurisdiction and a taxpayer but recognises that there could be changes to such an APA in a bilateral Mutual Agreement Procedure. See further paragraph 4.140 of these Guidelines, and in general Section F of Chapter IV of these Guidelines.

Appendix A – Relevant benchmarking search criteria

This Appendix describes the relevant benchmarking search criteria applied for the purposes of identifying companies involved in baseline marketing and distribution activities and relied upon to establish the global dataset which in part forms the basis for the approximation of arm's length results under the simplified and streamlined approach.

Database filtering

Moody's BvD Orbis database[1] was used for the initial research of defining relevant benchmarking search criteria and only the following criteria were considered initially.

1. Active companies
2. Companies with primary NACE codes 45 - Wholesale and retail trade and repair of motor vehicles and motorcycles and 46 - Wholesale trade except of motor vehicles and motorcycles[2]
3. Companies with consolidated accounts, or unconsolidated only where the company is known to own less than 50% of any subsidiaries
4. Companies with no shareholders with ownership of more than 50% of the shares of the company
5. Companies with operating revenue and EBIT data available for 2017, 2018 and 2019
6. Companies with operating revenue average of at least EUR 2 million for 5 years (2015-2019)
7. Companies with a website address
8. Companies with business overview information available in the database
9. Excluding companies with a research and development to sales ratio of more than 3%[3]

Manual review of company descriptions

After the filtering described above, a manual review of the companies was performed.

This review aimed at rejecting from the final dataset any companies undertaking more than baseline wholesale marketing and distribution activities based on scoping criteria outlined in Section 2.

---

[1] There are database license restrictions associated with the use and dissemination of detailed data and company information.

[2] Noting further refinements through the qualitative review outlined in the next section.

[3] This is an initial database search criteria, later refined through the manual rejection of companies described as carrying out research and development activities in their business descriptions and further quantitative filtering described below.

Initially, keyword searches were used to make rejections of companies, and then manually reviewed the companies in the dataset using only the descriptive information on businesses activities provided in the database.

This review comprised -

- Rejection of companies with the following terms in their business overview:
  - "design and manufactur",
  - "financ",
  - "insurance",
  - "manufacture ",
  - "research", "software d" and "system integrat".
- Rejection of all companies that do not describe wholesale distribution as their main activity.
- Rejection of companies which describe any development, research or manufacturing activity, or more than minority or ancillary levels of additional activities such as retail, repairs and maintenance, and other services.

Quantitative review of company data

Companies reporting a 5-year weighted average of intangible fixed assets to sales higher than 1% were rejected.

Of companies reporting a figure for research and development expenses those reporting a 5 year weighted average of R&D over sales of more than 0% were rejected.

Companies reporting losses in 3, 4 or 5 of the 5 years considered in this analysis were rejected as persistent loss makers.

Application of the commodities exemption

Companies remaining in the dataset have been subject to further high-level qualitative checks of company website and internet information to identify the products being distributed. Where a company is distributing products which meet the definition of commodity in this guidance, that company has been removed from the data set in line with the scoping exemption for commodities.

Appendix B – Illustrative examples

> The assumptions in the following numerical examples are intended for illustrative purposes only and should not be taken as prescribing adjustments and arm's length arrangements in actual cases or particular industries.
>
> While the examples seek to illustrate the interplay of the different components of the pricing methodology in section 5, the simplified and streamlined approach must be applied in each case according to the specific facts and circumstances.
>
> The illustrative examples use the midpoint for the adjustment under section 5.1, but any point within a range equal to the return on sales percentage derived from the pricing matrix (Table 5.1) plus or minus 0.5% can be relied upon for the purpose of demonstrating compliance with section 5.1.

1. The following 8 examples show how to calculate the return on sales of a tested party in scope of the simplified and streamlined approach. It assumes that the jurisdictions involved in the illustrations have implemented the simplified and streamlined approach, and that the tested party meets the scoping criteria, with no exclusions being applicable. Balance sheet items in the examples are calculated on an average basis in accordance with footnote 4 of the guidance.

Example 1 – Basic fact pattern with the industry Group 1 and the factor intensity classification [C]

2. Assume that GROUP AB is an MNE group that manufactures and distributes household consumables. Company A is the parent company of the group, resident in Country A. Company B is a subsidiary of GROUP AB resident in Country B that undertakes wholesale distribution activities in Country B.

3. Company A sells household consumables to Company B, who then sells the products, without further modifications, to third party retailers in Country B. Unless indicated otherwise in the examples, Country B is not a qualifying jurisdiction within the meaning of sections 5.2 and 5.3.

4. Assume Company B shows the following figures (before the calculation of the return under the simplified and streamlined approach):

a) Profit & loss of Company B in Year X-3 through Year X

		Year *X-3*	Year *X-2*	Year *X-1*	Year *X*
(a)	Sales	199	195	205	200
(b)	Cost of goods sold (COGS)	(145)	(142)	(154)	(144)
(c)= (a) + (b)	Gross profit	54	53	51	56
(d)	Operating expenses	(50)	(47)	(46)	(49)
(e)= (c) +(d)	Earnings Before Interest & Tax (EBIT)	4	6	5	7
(f) = (e) / (a)	***Return on Sales (%)***	***2.01%***	***3.08%***	***2.44%***	***3.50%***
(g) = (e) / (d)	***Return on Operating Expense***	***8.00%***	***12.77%***	***10.87%***	***14.29%***

b) Balance sheet items of Company B calculated on an average basis for Year X-3 through Year X-1

	Year *X-3*	Year *X-2*	Year *X-1*	Year *X*
Assets:				
Fixed assets	50	42	40	
Debtors	30	22	26	
Stock	25	18	25	
Liabilities:				
Creditors	33	34	36	

5. In order to determine the return of Company B in Year X under the simplified and streamlined approach, the following steps should be undertaken:

- **Step 1** – Determine the relevant industry grouping of the tested party.

  Company B falls into Group 1 of the industry groupings in the definitions section of the guidance.

- **Step 2** – Determine the relevant factor intensity classification.
  - As illustrated in the following tables, the net operating asset intensity of Company B calculated based on a weighted average of the preceding three-year period (from Year X-3 to Year X-1) is 29.22%, and the operating expenses intensity for the same period is 23.87%. Therefore, under the pricing matrix in section 5.1, the factor intensity classification of Company B is [C].
  - The account payable guardrail of 90 days under footnotes 5 and 29 of the guidance is not triggered as calculated in c).

c) Calculation of Accounts Payable guardrail

		Year *X-3*	Year *X-2*	Year *X-1*	Year *X*
(a)	Creditors	33	34	36	
(b)	COGS	145	142	154	
(c)= (a) / (b)	Ratio of Creditors to COGS	0.23	0.24	0.23	
(d)= (c) x 365	***Accounts payable days***	***83.07***	***87.39***	***85.32***	
(e)	Meet 90 days threshold	***Yes***	***Yes***	***Yes***	

d) Calculation of working capital in Year X-3 through Year X-1

		Year *X-3*	Year *X-2*	Year *X-1*	Year *X*
(a)	Stock	25	18	25	
(b)	Debtors	30	22	26	
(c)	Creditors	33	34	36	
(d)=(a)+(b)-(c)	Working capital	22	6	15	

e) Calculation of net operating assets intensity (OAS)

Net Operating assets

		Year *X-3*	Year *X-2*	Year *X-1*	Year *X*
(a)	Fixed assets	50	42	40	
(b)	Working capital	22	6	15	
(c)=(a)+(b)	Net Operating assets	72	48	55	

Net operating assets intensity (OAS)

		Year *X-3*	Year *X-2*	Year *X-1*	3-year weighted average
(a)	Sales	199	195	205	***599***
(b)	Net Operating assets	72	48	55	***175***
(c)=(b)/(a)	***OAS%***				***29.22%***

f) Calculation of operating expense intensity (OES)

		Year *X-3*	Year *X-2*	Year *X-1*	3-year weighted average
(a)	Sales	199	195	205	***599***
(b)	Operating expenses	50	47	46	***143***
(c)=(b)/(a)	***OES%***				***23.87%***

- **Step 3** –Identify and apply the range from the relevant matrix segment.

  Under the pricing matrix in section 5.1 the return of Company B in year X should be 2.5% (+/- 0.5%).
- **Step 4** – Apply the operating expense cross-check of section 5.2.

  The operating expense cross-check described in section 5.2 is not triggered because the equivalent return on operating expenses result (10.20%) is within the operating expense cap-and-collar range (10%-60%).
- **Step 5** – Apply data availability mechanism of section 5.3.

  Data availability mechanism described in Section 5.3 is not triggered because Country B is not a qualifying jurisdiction.

6. The table below illustrates the calculation of the operating margin of the tested party under the streamlined and simplified approach.

Year X			
		P&L *(before Section 5 calculation)*	**P&L *(after Section 5 calculation)***
(a)	Sales	200	200
(b)	Cost of Goods Sold	(144)	(146)
(c)= (a) + (b)	Gross profit	56	54
(d)	Operating expenses	(49)	(49)
(e)= (c) + (d)	Earnings Before Interest & Tax (EBIT)	7	5
(f)= (e) / (a)	***Return on Sales (%)***	***3.5%***	
(g)= (e) / (d)	***Return on Opex***	***14.29%***	
(h)	***RoS% under Section 5.1***		***2.5%***
(i)= (a) x (h)	***EBIT under Section 5.1***		***5***
(j)= (i) / (d)	***Equivalent return on OPEX***		***10.20%***

Example 2 – Basic fact pattern with the industry Group 3 and the factor intensity classification [D]

7. The facts are the same as in Example 1 except the figures of the profit & loss and balance sheet items calculated on an average basis of Company B in Year X-3 through Year X have changed as follows, and the MNE group produces and sells medical machinery.

a) Profit & loss of Company B in Year X-3 through Year X

		Year *X-3*	Year *X-2*	Year *X-1*	Year *X*
(a)	Sales	199	195	205	200
(b)	Cost of goods sold (COGS)	(156)	(163)	(164)	(156)
(c)= (a) + (b)	Gross profit	43	32	41	44
(d)	Operating expenses	(37)	(26)	(33)	(36)
(e)= (c) + (d)	Earnings Before Interest & Tax (EBIT)	6	6	8	8
(f) = (e) / (a)	***Return on Sales (%)***	***3.02%***	***3.08%***	***3.90%***	***4.00%***
(g) = (e) / (d)	***Return on Operating Expense***	***16.22%***	***23.08%***	***24.24%***	***22.22%***

b) Balance sheet items of Company B calculated on an average basis for Year X-3 through Year X-1

	Year *X-3*	Year *X-2*	Year *X-1*	Year *X*
Assets:				
Fixed assets	26	28	22	
Debtors	15	18	22	
Stock	20	16	20	
Liabilities:				
Creditors	33	36	35	

8. In order to determine the return of Company B in Year X under the simplified and streamlined approach, the following steps should be undertaken:

- **Step 1 and Step 2 –** Company B falls into Group 3 of the industry groupings and the factor intensity classification of Company B is [D] as illustrated in the table c). The account payable guardrail of 90 days under footnotes 5 and 29 of the guidance is not triggered.

c) Working capital, Net operating assets, OAS% and OES%

	Year *X-3*	Year *X-2*	Year *X-1*	3-year weighted average
Working capital	**2**	**(2)**	**7**	**-**
Net Operating assets	**28**	**26**	**29**	**-**
OAS%	**-**	**-**	**-**	**13.86%**
OES%	**-**	**-**	**-**	**16.03%**

- **Step 3 – Step 5 –** Under the pricing matrix in section 5.1, the return of Company B in year X should be 3 % (+/- 0.5%). The operating expense cross-check described in section 5.2 is not triggered because the equivalent return on operating expenses result (16.67%) is within the operating expense cap-and-collar range (10%-40%), and Data availability mechanism described in Section 5.3 is not triggered because Country B is not a qualifying jurisdiction.

9. The table below illustrates the calculation of the operating margin of the tested party under the streamlined and simplified approach.

Year X			
		P&L *(before Section 5 calculation)*	**P&L** *(after Section 5 calculation)*
(a)	Sales	200	200
(b)	Cost of Goods Sold	(156)	(158)
(c)= (a) + (b)	Gross profit	44	42.00
(d)	Operating expenses	(36)	(36)
(e)= (c) + (d)	Earnings Before Interest & Tax (EBIT)	8	6
(f)= (e) / (a)	***Return on Sales (%)***	***4.00%***	
(g)= (e) / (d)	***Return on Opex***	***22.22%***	
(h)	***RoS% under Section 5.1***		***3.00%***
(i)= (a) x (h)	***EBIT under Section 5.1***		***6.00***
(j)= (i) / (d)	***Equivalent return on OPEX***		***16.67%***

Example 3 – Application of the Data availability mechanism for qualifying jurisdictions

10. The facts are the same as in Example 2 except that Country B is a qualifying jurisdiction within the meaning of sections 5.2 (operating expense cross-check) and 5.3 (the data availability mechanism) and has a sovereign credit rating for the relevant fiscal year of BB-.

11. As in Example 2, the operating expense cross-check described in section 5.2 is not triggered because the equivalent return on operating expenses result (16.67%) is within the operating expense cap-and-collar range (10%-45%).

12. In accordance with the data availability mechanism, Company B will earn an adjusted return in accordance with the following formula:

$$\text{Adjusted return on sales} = ROS^{TP} + (NRA^{J} \times OAS^{TP})$$

13. ROS^{TP} is 3% (the return on sales percentage of the tested party calculated in accordance with Sections 5.1 and 5.2 where applicable), NRA^{J} is 1.8% (the net risk adjustment percentage of a jurisdiction with the sovereign credit rating with BB-) and OAS^{TP} is 13.86% [4](the net operating asset intensity percentage of Company B based on weighted average of year X-3 to X-1). The table below illustrates adjusted return on sales for Company B after application of the data availability mechanism.

Year X		
(a)	RoS% under Section 5.1	3%
(b)	Net Risk Adjustment%	1.80%
(c)	OAS%	13.86%
(d)= (a) + ((b) x (c))	**Adjusted RoS% under Section 5.3**	**3.25%**

Example 4 – Opex cross-check cap is triggered

14. The facts are the same as in Example 2 except the figures of the profit & loss in Year X-3 through Year X and balance sheet items calculated on an average basis of Company B in Year X-3 through Year X-1 have changed as follows, and the MNE group produces and sells consumer electronics:

[4] Net operating asset guardrail of 85% under Section 5.3 is not exceeded.

a) Profit & loss of Company B in Year X-3 through Year X

		Year X-3	Year X-2	Year X-1	Year X
(a)	Sales	199	195	205	200
(b)	Cost of goods sold (COGS)	(181)	(178)	(187)	(182)
(c)= (a) + (b)	Gross profit	18	17	18	18
(d)	Operating expenses	(11)	(11)	(11)	(10)
(e)= (c) +(d)	Earnings Before Interest & Tax (EBIT)	7	6	7	8
(f) = (e) / (a)	***Return on Sales (%)***	***3.52%***	***3.08%***	***3.41%***	***4.00%***
(g) = (e) / (d)	***Return on Operating Expense***	***63.64%***	***54.55%***	***63.64%***	***80.00%***

b) Balance sheet items of Company B calculated on an average basis for Year X-3 through Year X-1

	Year X-3	Year X-2	Year X-1	Year X
Assets:				
Fixed assets	48	42	45	
Debtors	31	37	33	
Stock	20	16	20	
Liabilities:				
Creditors	33	36	35	

15. In order to determine the return of Company B in Year X under the simplified and streamlined approach, the following steps should be undertaken:

- **Step 1 and Step 2 –** Company B falls into Group 2 of the industry groupings and the factor intensity classification of Company B is [B] as illustrated in the table c). The account payable guardrail of 90 days under footnotes 5 and 29 of the guidance is not triggered.

c) Working capital, Net operating assets, OAS% and OES%

	Year X-3	Year X-2	Year X-1	3-year weighted average
Working capital	**18**	**17**	**18**	**-**
Net Operating assets	**66**	**59**	**63**	**-**
OAS%	**-**	**-**	**-**	**31.39%**
OES%	**-**	**-**	**-**	**5.51%**

- **Step 3 –** Under the pricing matrix in Section 5.1, the return of Company B in year X should be 3.75 % (+/- 0.5%).
- **Step 4** – The operating expense cross-check described in Section 5.2 is triggered because the equivalent return on operating expenses result (75.00%) exceeds the operating expense cap-and-collar range (10%-60%). Since the equivalent return on operating expenses exceeds the range, the return on sales of Company B will be adjusted downwards until it results in the equivalent return on operating expenses equal to the operating expense cap. The return on sales after the adjustment is 3.00%.
- **Step 5 –** Data availability mechanism described in Section 5.3 is not triggered because Country B is not a qualifying jurisdiction.

16. The table below illustrates the calculation of the operating margin of the tested party under the streamlined and simplified approach.

	Year X			
		P&L ***(before Section 5 calculation)***	**P&L** ***(after Section 5.1 calculation)***	**P&L** ***(after Section 5.2 calculation)***
(a)	Sales	200	200	200
(b)	Cost of Goods Sold	(182)	(182.5)	(184)
(c)= (a) + (b)	Gross profit	18	17.5	16
(d)	Operating expenses	(10)	(10)	(10)
(e)= (c) + (d)	Earnings Before Interest & Tax (EBIT)	8	7.5	6
(f)= (e) / (a)	**Return on Sales (%)**	**4.00%**		
(g)= (e) / (d)	**Return on OPEX**	**80.00%**		
(h)	**RoS% under Section 5.1**		**3.75%**	
(i)= (a) x (h)	**EBIT under Section 5.1**		**7.5**	
(j)= (i) / (d)	**Equivalent return on OPEX**		**75.00%**	
(k)= (d) x 60%	**Adjusted EBIT under Section 5.2**			**6**
(l)= (k) / (a)	**Adj. Return on Sales (%) under Section 5.2**			**3.00%**

Example 5 - Application of the Opex cross-check and Data availability mechanism

17. The facts are the same as in Example 4 except Country B is a qualifying jurisdiction within the meaning of Sections 5.2 (operating expense cross-check) and 5.3 (the data availability mechanism) and has a sovereign credit rating for the relevant fiscal year of B-.

18. As in Example 4, the operating expense cross-check described in Section 5.2 is triggered because the equivalent return on operating expenses result (75.00%) exceeds the operating expense cap-and-collar range (10%-70%). Since the equivalent return on operating expenses exceeds the range, the return on sales of Company B will be adjusted downwards until it results in the equivalent return on operating expenses equal to the operating expense cap. The return on sales after the adjustment is 3.50%.

19. In accordance with the data availability mechanism, Company B will earn an adjusted return in accordance with the following formula:

$$\text{Adjusted return on sales} = ROS^{TP} + (NRA^{J} \times OAS^{TP})$$

20. ROS^{TP} is 3.50% (the return on sales after an adjustment based on Section 5.2), NRA^{J} is 4.9% (the net risk adjustment percentage of a jurisdiction with the sovereign credit rating with B-) and OAS^{TP} is 31.39% [5](the net operating asset intensity percentage of the Company B based on weighted average of year X-3 to X-1). The table below illustrates adjusted return on sales for Company B after application of the data availability mechanism.

	Year X	
(a)	RoS% under Section 5.1 and 5.2	3.50%
(b)	Net Risk Adjustment%	4.90%
(c)	OAS%	31.39%
(d)= (a) + ((b) x (c))	**Adjusted RoS% under Section 5.3**	**5.04%**

[5] Net operating asset guardrail of 85% under Section 5.3 is not exceeded.

Example 6 – NOA accounts payable days guardrail is exceeded

21. The facts are the same as in Example 4 except the figures of the profit & loss and balance sheet items calculated on an average basis of Company B in Year X-3 through Year X-1 have changed as follows and the account payable guardrail of 90 days under footnotes 5 and 29 of the guidance is exceeded.

a) *Profit & loss of Company B in Year X-3 through Year X*

		Year *X-3*	Year *X-2*	Year *X-1*	Year *X*
(a)	Sales	199	185	195	200
(b)	Cost of goods sold (COGS)	(181)	(168)	(177)	(182)
(c)= (a) + (b)	Gross profit	18	17	18	18
(d)	Operating expenses	(11)	(11)	(11)	(10)
(e)= (c) +(d)	Earnings Before Interest & Tax (EBIT)	7	6	7	8
(f) = (e) / (a)	***Return on Sales (%)***	***3.52%***	***3.24%***	***3.59%***	***4.00%***

b) *balance sheet items of Company B calculated on an average basis for Year X-3 through Year X-1*

	Year *X-3*	Year *X-2*	Year *X-1*	Year *X*
Assets:				
Fixed assets	48	42	45	
Debtors	31	39	39	
Stock	36	28	20	
Liabilities:				
Creditors	65	65	55	

22. In order to determine the return of Company B in Year X under the simplified and streamlined approach, the following steps should be undertaken:

- **Step 1** – Company B falls into Group 2 of the industry groupings in the definitions section of the guidance.
- **Step 2** – the factor intensity classification of Company B is [B] as illustrated in the table e). Since the account payable guardrail of 90 days under footnotes 5 and 29 of the guidance applies and creditors are adjusted, working capital and net operating assets intensity (OAS) should be calculated with the adjusted creditors.

c) *Calculation of Accounts Payable guardrail*

		Year *X-3*	Year *X-2*	Year *X-1*	Year *X*
(a)	Creditors	65	65	55	
(b)	Cost of Goods Sold	181	168	177	
(c)= (a) / (b)	**Ratio of Creditors to COGS**	**0.36**	**0.39**	**0.31**	
(d)= (c) x 365	**Accounts payable days**	**131.08**	**141.22**	**113.42**	
(e)	**Meet 90-day threshold**	**No**	**No**	**No**	
(f)= [(b) / 365] x 90	**Adj. creditors**	**44.63**	**41.42**	**43.64**	
(g)= (f) / (b)	**Adj. ratio of Creditors to COGS**	**0.25**	**0.25**	**0.25**	
(h)= (g) x 365	**Adj. accounts payable days**	**90 days**	**90 days**	**90 days**	

d) Adjusted Balance sheet items of Company B calculated on an average basis as a result of Accounts Payable guardrail

	Year *X-3*	Year *X-2*	Year *X-1*	Year *X*
Assets:				
Fixed assets	48	42	45	
Debtors	31	39	39	
Stock	36	28	20	
Liabilities:				
Creditors	44.63	41.42	43.64	

e) Working capital and Net operating asset, OAS% and OES%

	Year *X-3*	Year *X-2*	Year *X-1*	3-year weighted average
Working capital with adjusted creditors	**22.37**	**25.58**	**15.36**	**-**
Net Operating assets with adjusted creditors	**70.37**	**67.58**	**60.36**	**-**
Unadjusted OAS%	**-**	**-**	**-**	**24.70%**
Adjusted OAS%	**-**	**-**	**-**	**34.25%**
OES%	**-**	**-**	**-**	**5.70%**

- Step 3 – Under the pricing matrix in Section 5.1 the return of Company B in year X should be 3.75 % (+/- 0.5%).
- **Step 4** – The operating expense cross-check described in Section 5.2 is triggered because the equivalent return on operating expenses result (75.00%) exceeds the operating expense cap-and-collar range (10%-60%). Since the equivalent return on operating expenses exceeds the range, the return on sales of Company B will be adjusted downwards until it results in the equivalent return on operating expenses equal to the operating expense cap. The return on sales after the adjustment is 3.0%.
- **Step 5** – Data availability mechanism described in Section 5.3 is not triggered because Country B is not a qualifying jurisdiction.

The table below illustrates the calculation of the operating margin of the tested party under the streamlined and simplified approach.

		Year X		
		P&L ***(before Section 5 calculation)***	**P&L** ***(after Section 5.1 calculation)***	**P&L** ***(after Section 5.2 calculation)***
(a)	Sales	200	200	200
(b)	Cost of Goods Sold	(182)	(182.5)	(184)
(c)= (a) + (b)	Gross profit	18	17.5	16
(d)	Operating expenses	(10)	(10)	(10)
(e)= (c) + (d)	Earnings Before Interest & Tax (EBIT)	8	7.5	6
(f)= (e) / (a)	**Return on Sales (%)**	4.0%		
(g)= (e) / (d)	**Return on OPEX**	80.00%		
(h)	**RoS% under Section 5.1**		3.75%	
(i)= (a) x (h)	**EBIT under Section 5.1**		7.5	
(j)= (i) / (d)	**Equivalent return on OPEX**		75.00%	
(k)= (d) x 60%	**Adjusted EBIT under Section 5.2**			6
(l)= (k) / (a)	**Adj. Return on Sales (%) under Section 5.2**			3.00%

Example 7 – Multiple industry grouping where de minimis threshold of 20% of sales is exceeded

23. The facts are the same as in Example 1 except the MNE group produces and sells both household consumables and electrical components and consumables, and in year X, Company B earns 60% of sales from selling household consumables and 40% of sales from selling electrical components and consumables.

24. Since Company B sells goods falling in to more than one industry group (household consumables in industry group 1 and electrical components and consumables in industry group 2) and the de minimis threshold of 20% of sales is exceeded for both industry groupings, calculation of a weighted average return is required as the table below illustrates.

Profit & loss extract of Company B in Year X

Year X segmented P&L			
	Total	***industry group 1 Category [C]***	***industry group 2 category [C]***
Sales	200	120	80
Shares in total sales		***60%***	***40%***
RoS% under Section 5.1	*(60% x 2.50%) + (40% x 3.00%)* **= *2.70% (+/- 0.5%)***		

Example 8 – Multiple industry grouping where de minimis threshold of 20% of sales is not met.

25. The facts are same as in example 7 except that in year X, Company B earns 93% of sales from selling household consumables and 7% of sales from selling electrical components and consumables.

26. Although Company B sells goods falling in to more than one industry group (household consumables in industry group 1 and electrical components and consumables in industry group 2), calculation of a weighted average return is not required because the de minimis threshold of 20% of sales is not met for industry grouping 2.

Profit & loss extract of Company B in Year X

Year X segmented P&L			
	Total	***industry group 1 Category [C]***	***Industry group 2 category [C]***
Sales	200	186	14
Share in total sales		***93%***	***7%***
RoS% under Section 5.1	100% x 2.50% = 2.50% (+/- 0.5%)		

www.ingramcontent.com/pod-product-compliance
Lightning Source LLC
Chambersburg PA
CBHW061225240926
51846CB00006B/1364
* 9 7 8 9 2 6 4 9 3 3 1 9 4 *